My grandparents taught me to never give up and to always chase my dreams, no matter what.

My mom did the most selfless act and gave me the ultimate opportunity for survival, against all odds.

This is for them.

ISBN 979-8-218-44831-8 (paperback)
ISBN 979-8-218-49904-4 (hardcover)

Book design by Arlene Soto

What *IS* That?

writtten by Ashley Hamblin
illustrated by Samantha Fistere

Meet Ashley and her grandparents! She's just like you and me!

When she was born, she was the size of a newborn puppy and weighed less than a football!

Because she was so small, Ashley does not walk or eat like you and needs help! Have you ever seen a wheelchair? How about a feeding tube or arm crutches?

You may be asking, **"What is that?"**

Let's go find out!

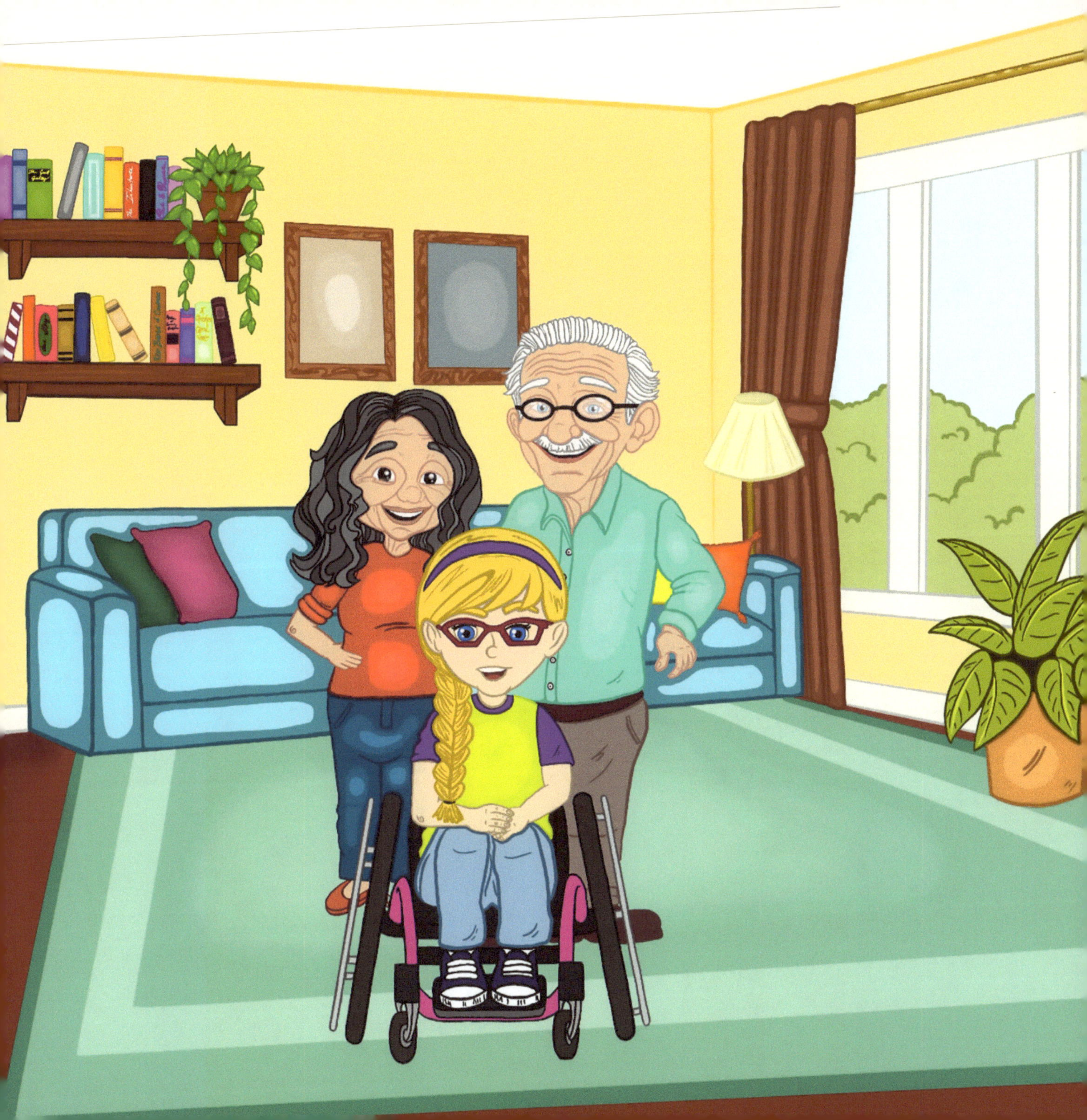

"What is that?" Ella asks her dad, seeing a pink wheelchair roll by at the park.

"That's a **wheelchair**, Ella," her dad says, smiling.

"Why does she need it?" Ella questions, confused.

"Would you like to go ask?"

Ella nods happily.

"Excuse me, miss?" Ella's dad asks. Ashley smiles and waves.

"Do you mind if my daughter asks you a question about your wheelchair?" Ella happily waves back.

"Hi!" Ashley says in a happy voice. "What's your question?"

"Why do you need a wheelchair?" Ella asks.

"Your legs help you get around, right?" Ashley replies. Ella nods.

"My legs have a mind of their own and don't work like yours. My wheelchair helps me get around!" Ashley says.

"I'm going to tell my friend Alex!" Ella is excited to learn something new!

"Mommy!" Ryan says. **"*What is that?*"** he asks, looking at Ashley's walking sticks.

"Those are called **arm crutches**," his mom replies.

"Why does she need them?" Ryan is confused.

"Let's go ask her ourselves, okay?" his mom says, smiling. Ryan is nervous.

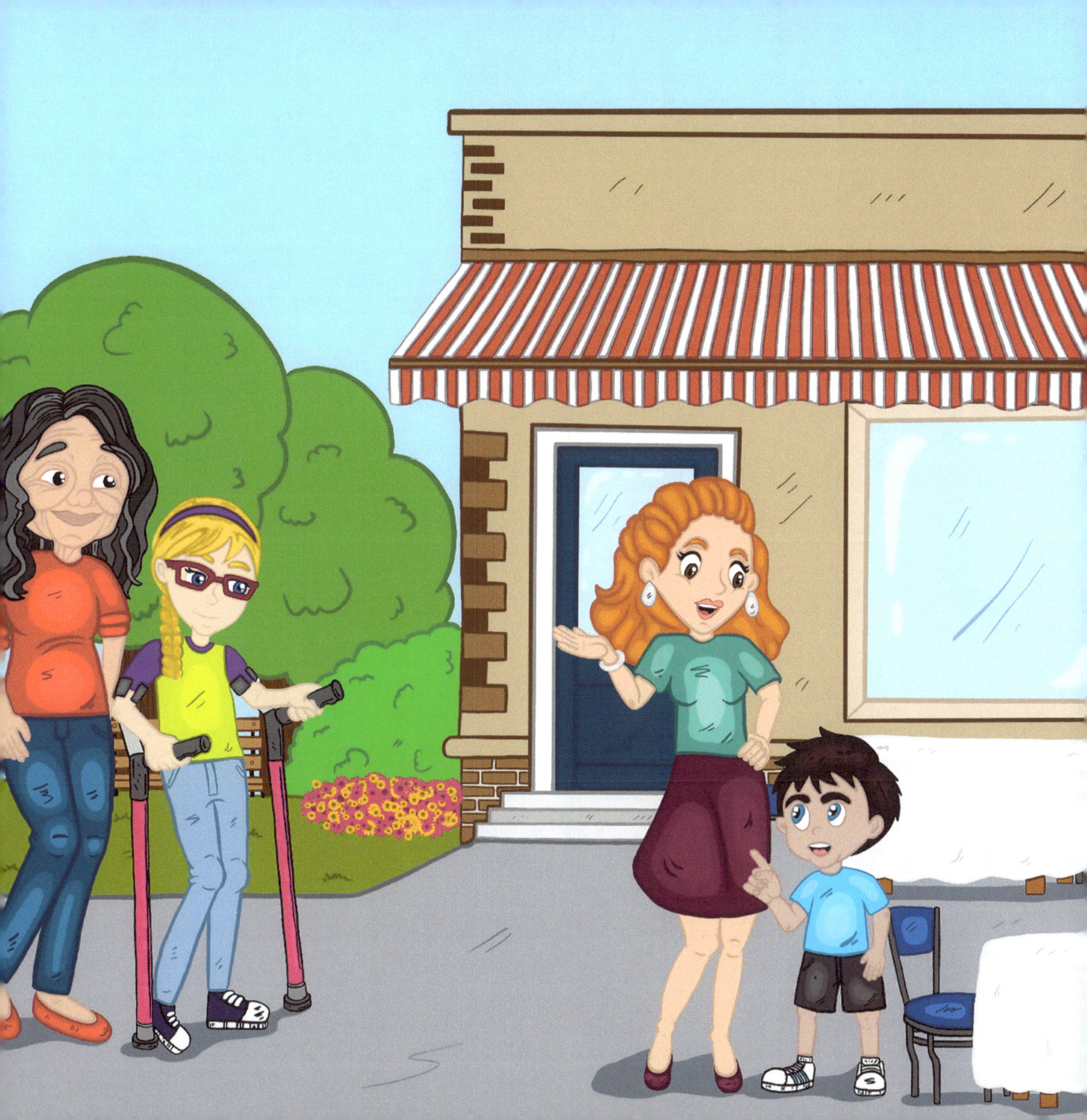

"Do you mind if my son asks you a question?" his mom asks, smiling at Ashley and her grandmother.

"Not at all!" Ashley says. "What's your question?"

"Why do you need those?" Ryan asks, looking at the pink arm crutches.

"These help me walk short distances!" Ashley says, picking up one arm crutch with a smile.

"That's so cool! I'm going to tell my brother!" Ryan is happy.

"Sissy, **what is that?**" Caitlyn asks, looking at the object in Ashley's tummy.

"That's called a **feeding tube**, Cait," her sister says, watching Ashley build a sandcastle.

"Why does she need it?" Caitlyn whispers.

"Do you want to ask her yourself?"

Caitlyn nods. She is curious.

"Do you mind if my sister asks you a question?"
Caitlyn's sister asks.

"Not at all!" Ashley says. "What's the question?"

"Why do you have that?" Caitlyn has never seen a feeding tube.

"This little guy helps me stay healthy by giving me medicine and
helping me eat!" Ashley smiles.

"That's neat! I'm going to tell my mommy!" Caitlyn says.

"Aunt Brandy, **what is that?**" Lucas asks, watching Ashley's grandfather carry a red object into his house.

"That's called a **walker**, Lucas," his aunt replies.

"Like grandma uses?" Lucas wonders.

"How about we go ask him ourselves?" his aunt says.

WELCO

"What are you carrying?" Lucas asks.
Ashley's grandfather smiles.

"This is a walker!" he replies.

"Why do you need it?" Lucas wonders.

"My granddaughter's legs do not work like ours," he says.
"When she was little, this used to help her go places!"

"I'm telling my nana!" Lucas says. "That's so cool!"

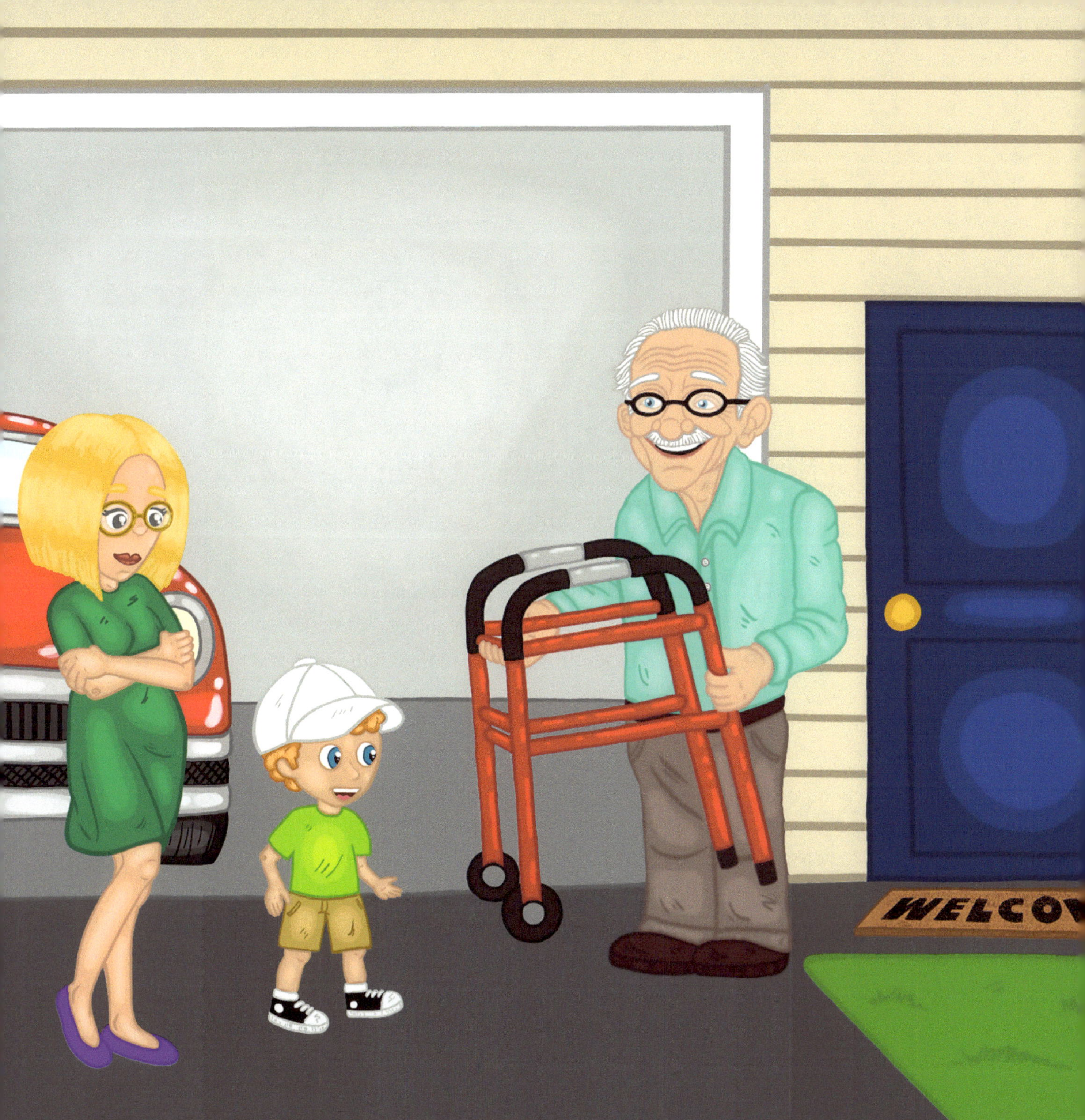

WELCO

"Alex!" Ella is excited to tell her friend what she saw.
"I saw a pink **wheelchair** today!" she says.

"What is that?" her friend asks. He is curious.

"It helps my new friend go places!" she says, coloring.

"Frankie!" Ryan yells. "Guess what I saw?"

"What?" his brother asks, eating macaroni and cheese.

"I saw **arm crutches**!" Ryan is excited.

"What is that?" Frankie does not understand.

"They look like sticks, but they're not!" Ryan says.

"What do they do?" Frankie asks with a smile and a curious face.

"They help my friend walk different places!" Ryan replies.

"I saw a **feeding tube** at the beach!" Caitlyn tells her mom, playing in her room.

"Really?" Her mom is excited for her. **"What is that?"**

"It's in her tummy!" Caitlyn says.

"What does it do?" Her mom asks.

"It helps her eat and take medicine!" Caitlyn is happy. She thinks of her new friend the rest of the day.

"Nana! Guess what I saw!" Lucas says. He is excited.

"What did you see?" his nana asks, sitting on the couch.

"I saw a **walker**!" Lucas says happily, playing with his toys.
"It was red!" red was his favorite color.

"Wow!" his nana is excited for him. **"What is that?"**

"It helped my friend go places when she was little!" Lucas says.

"I learned something," Ella says, cuddling her teddy bear and getting ready for bed.

"What did you learn?" her mom asks.

"That my friend is no different than me just because she does not walk or eat like I do!" Ella says.

"That's right!" her mom says.

"What do I say if someone says, *'What is that?'* when they see her wheelchair?" Ella is confused. "What if they point?"

"They may be curious like you were," her mom replies. "Tell them what a wheelchair is and what it is used for, just as you learned!"

Ella yawns. She is tired.

"Goodnight," her mom says, turning out her light.

About the Author

Meet Ashley! She's an adventurous soul with Cerebral Palsy, using her wheelchair and other cool gadgets to explore the world. Given a 0% chance of survival by her doctors, Ashley has proved them all wrong! Today, she's helping kids and grown-ups understand the world of disability and why inclusion is so important.

Join her adventure at www.ashleysvantage.com!

Did you enjoy the book?

Remember to leave a review on Amazon!